WOMEN
WHO MADE
HISTORY

ADVENTURERS
AND ATHLETES

Written by

JULIA ADAMS

Illustrated by

LOUISE WRIGHT

Gareth Stevens
PUBLISHING

Serena Williams
(page 13)

Please visit our website, www.garethstevens.com. For a free color catalog of all our high-quality books, call toll free 1-800-542-2595 or fax 1-877-542-2596.

Cataloging-in-Publication Data

Names: Adams, Julia. | Wright, Louise.
Title: Adventurers and athletes / Julia Adams, illustrated by Louise Wright.
Description: New York : Gareth Stevens Publishing, 2020.
| Series: Women who made history | Includes glossary and index.
Identifiers: ISBN 9781538243121 (pbk.) | ISBN 9781538243138 (library bound)
Subjects: LCSH: Women athletes–Biography–Juvenile literature.
| Women explorers–Biography–Juvenile literature.
Classification: LCC GV697.A1 A33 2020 | DDC 796.092'52 B–dc23

First Edition

Published in 2020 by
Gareth Stevens Publishing
111 East 14th Street, Suite 349
New York, NY 10003

Copyright © Arcturus Holdings Ltd, 2020

Author: Julia Adams
Illustrator: Louise Wright
Designer: Sally Bond
Editor: Susannah Bailey

Printed in the United States of America

CPSIA compliance information: Batch #CS19GS: For further information contact Gareth Stevens, New York, New York at 1-800-542-2595.

Marina Rascova
(page 23)

CONTENTS

Amelia Earhart
(page 38)

AWESOME WOMEN

Anne Bonny (page 19)

The course of history is packed with stories of women overcoming odds, defying expectations, and shattering stereotypes. Yet, all too often, their contribution has been overlooked, underplayed, or just forgotten.

Many cultures have believed (or still believe) that women do not need an education, cannot be trusted with leadership, are physically inferior, and are intellectually weak. Men have been privileged, and this means that they have been the world's default decision-makers and

Misty Copeland (page 26)

history writers. Women, however, have been achieving greatness even when everything seemed against them.

The adventurers and athletes in this book are by no means the definitive list of female historymakers, nor are they perfect and without fault, but they are pioneers who stood out, made a difference, and proved without a doubt that they were just as capable as men. Their contributions, both to their field and as an inspiration to others, are worthy of celebration. And that is what this book aims to do.

Junko Tabei
(page 36)

ADVENTURERS AND ATHLETES

Yusra Mardini (page 16)

History books are packed with real-life male action heroes—explorers, generals, spies, and sports stars—but where are the female ones? Many women have excelled in these areas, often against all odds.

The energetic high achievers in this book went above and beyond to prove their power. Whether they were floating in space, scaling a mountain, steering a faulty plane over the ocean,

Sacagawea
(page 28)

or redefining a whole sport, they faced challenges with courage. They believed in themselves, and that made anything possible. Sometimes these women risked their lives for their ideals. Some crossed enemy lines with fake identities to help their countries win a war—and they all refused to shrink their ambitions to fit silly notions of feminine frailty.

Some overcame disabilities to win medal after medal in Paralympian sports—showing us, in the process, that physical prowess has a lot to do with attitude. By boldly ignoring all those restrictive rules about what women can and cannot do, these extraordinary role models have opened up the world to us all.

Chantal Petitclerck
(page 32)

MAKING HISTORY

Who do you think of when you picture a great adventurer?
Christopher Colombus? How about when you think of a great
sportsperson? Usain Bolt? Lionel Messi? Or perhaps you think
of Jessica Ennis, a gold-medal–winning heptathlete? Well,
there are all sorts of women who fall into this
category along with the men. These pages are going to
introduce you to many brave and inspiring female
athletes and adventurers.

IDA PFEIFFER
(1797 – 1858)

Born in Vienna, Austria, Ida was treated in exactly the same way as her many brothers: she wore boys' clothes, had the same education, and was encouraged to be physically strong and independent. She dreamed of far-off places after a childhood trip to Palestine and Egypt.

Ida married and had a family. Once her sons had grown up and had families of their own, she was free.

She decided to travel. First she went to Turkey, Jerusalem, and Egypt. She published her memories of the trip and used the money for a trip to Iceland. Ida journeyed around the world twice. Her trips could last months or even years, and she paid for them by publishing her travel journals. She also sold specimens of animals, plants, and minerals.

VERA ATKINS

(1908-2000)

Born in Romania, Vera Maria Rosenberg moved to Britain with her parents in 1933. Her mother was English and Vera later took her English maiden name, Atkins. She was educated well in England and France, studying modern languages.

When World War II broke out, Vera joined the Women's Auxiliary Air Force. Later she went to work at "Section F." This was an important branch of the Special Operations Executive, an organization set up to run secret operations in occupied countries. Her job was recruiting spies to gather intelligence in France. She became deputy and assistant to the head of the SOE and was vital to its operations.

Vera was a key secret agent of World War II. She was dedicated to her work and had a strong sense of duty. After the war, she visited France in person to find out what had happened to British agents who went missing there.

"I could not just abandon their memory," she said. "I decided we must find out what happened to each one, and where."

MARTA

SOCCER PLAYER

(b.1986)

Far in the northeast of the country, Alagoas is one of Brazil's most disadvantaged states. More than one-fifth of its people cannot read or write, the hospitals are understaffed and overcrowded, its industries are declining, and water supplies and sanitation are limited.

Marta Vieira da Silva was born and grew up in Alagoas. Her father left when she was a year old, and her mother went out to work full-time as a cleaner.

Home alone with her two brothers and sister, Marta discovered soccer. She played out on the street without shoes and kicked a ball made of scrunched up plastic bags. When Marta was five, her mother refused to buy her a ball, saying "You're a girl, Marta." But Marta did not accept that soccer was just for boys. By the age of seven, she was training with the boys every day.

Marta couldn't attend school regularly because of her family's money problems. From the age of 11, she worked as a street vendor selling fruit and clothes and also played for her local soccer club.

"There may be tough times, but the difficulties which you face will make you more determined to achieve your objectives and to win against all the odds."

When Marta was 14 years old, she was spotted by soccer scout and coach Helena Pacheco. Marta made a three-day bus trip to Rio de Janeiro to join the Vasco da Gama club.

Marta represented Brazil in the 2002 under-20 Women's World Cup and she moved up to the national squad the following year. She was voted Fifa Women's World Player of the Year five years running from 2006 to 2010.

In the 2007 Women's World Cup, Marta won the Golden Ball for best player and Golden Boot as top scorer. She has won silver medals in two Olympics and was disappointed to be knocked out in the semifinals at the 2016 Rio Games.

Marta has played for clubs in Europe and the United States, as well as Brazil. She reached the final of the UEFA Women's Cup (now the Women's Champions League) twice with Swedish club Umeå IK.

Marta is considered the best female soccer player in history, celebrated for her skill, speed, and finesse. She had to be tough to make it in Brazil, a country where the women's game was banned from 1941 to 1979 for being unfeminine.

FIFA WOMEN'S PLAYER OF THE YEAR

Women's soccer still faces huge inequality. A 2017 survey found that top male player Neymar, who is from Brazil like Marta, earned the same as all 1,693 players in the top seven women's football leagues combined. His salary from Paris Saint-Germain FC was 1,150 times more than Marta's from Orlando Pride. There is still a long, long way to go.

VENUS WILLIAMS
TENNIS PLAYER
(b.1980)

Long before Venus Ebone Starr Williams was born, her father Richard dreamed of having a child who was a tennis star. He saw the sport as a path out of poverty—a way to break free from the ghetto. He and his wife Oracene learned all about the game from books and videos. When their four-year-old daughter Venus showed promise, they began to coach her on local public courts. Soon Venus's younger sister Serena joined in the training. The girls gave each other support and healthy competition.

"When you lose, you're more motivated. When you win, you fail to see your mistakes and probably no one can tell you anything."

By the age of ten, Venus could serve a ball at 100 miles (160 km) per hour, and at 14 she took up tennis professionally. Venus's debut at the US Open was in 1997. She ranked only 66th in the world but reached the final—the first unseeded player to do so.

In 2000, Venus won two Grand Slams (Wimbledon and the US Open) and two Olympic gold medals (for the women's singles and doubles) in Sydney, Australia.

Venus stayed at the top of her game for years in spite of injuries and having to cope with an autoimmune disease. She wasn't the first African American to win a Grand Slam—Althea Gibson achieved that in 1956—but she ushered in a new, powerful way of playing. Venus succeeded by trusting her own individuality, and that makes her an example for people in all walks of life, not just tennis.

WIMBLEDON TROPHY

SERENA WILLIAMS
Tennis Player
(b.1981)

Born 15 months after her sister Venus, Serena Jameka Williams has profited from her parents' determination to make their daughters tennis stars. She was included in her sister's training sessions, and the girls started entering tennis tournaments when Serena was five years old.

One year after Venus became a professional player, Serena followed in her footsteps. She went on to win the US Open in 1999, a year before her big sister. However, her real breakthrough year was 2002, when she won a Grand Slam hat trick—the French Open, US Open, and Australian Open.

Winning the Olympic gold and all four Grand Slam tournaments is known as a Career Golden Slam. In 2002, Serena became the second woman to achieve one in the singles (Steffi Graf was the first). Playing in the doubles, the Williams sisters have completed two Career Golden Slams!

Serena's win at the 2017 Australian Open took her total Grand Slam singles titles to a record-breaking 23. The victory was all the more extraordinary because she was eight weeks pregnant at the time.

Like Venus, Serena plays with a forceful, athletic style. Her career has been inspirational, especially to young black players.

"The success of every woman should be the inspiration to another. We should raise each other up."

AUSTRALIAN OPEN TROPHY

BESSIE COLEMAN
Aviator
(1892–1926)

Texas still had segregation laws when Bessie Coleman was born there in 1892. It was nearly 30 years since slavery had been abolished, but many white people still held racist views and often treated black people as inferior.

Bessie was the 10th of 13 children. Her father was mixed race (Cherokee and African American) and her mother was African American. They were farmhands. Bessie helped out in the fields, but she also had an education. She went to a segregated school and had one term at the African American university in Langston, Oklahoma.

When she was 23, Bessie went to live in Chicago and worked as a nail technician. She became fascinated by flying. Newspapers were full of stories about the brave pilots returning from World War I. Aviation was still very new. The first powered flight had only happened in 1903.

No American flying school would take Bessie because she was mixed race and a woman. She got the idea of going to France, where there was less discrimination, from Robert Abbott, who ran Chicago's biggest black newspaper. He and Jesse Binga, owner of Chicago's first African American bank, helped to fund Bessie's trip.

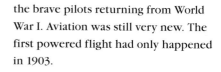

Bessie went to the best flight school in France at Le Crotoy. Aircraft were dangerously flimsy in those early days and some of Bessie's fellow students died during training.

In June 1921, Bessie earned her international pilot's license. She was the first black woman pilot. Bessie decided to make a living as a barnstormer, or stunt pilot. Barnstorming was a popular entertainment in the 1920s.

On September 3, 1922, Bessie took part in an air show on Long Island, New York. It was the first of many. A skilled and dedicated pilot, Bessie wowed audiences by flying upside down, rolling, diving, and looping-the-loop. She became known as "Queen Bessie."

"The air is the only place free from prejudices."

Bessie wanted to break down racial barriers. She refused to perform to segregated audiences and she also gave talks about aviation to African Americans in churches, halls, and schools. She was saving up to start the first black flying school when she tragically died in 1926. She fell to her death during a rehearsal for a stunt show and her mechanic also died in the accident. Thousands came to Bessie's funeral to pay their respects. To this day, African American pilots mark the anniversary of her death by flying over her grave and dropping flowers.

Bessie's dream of a black flight school did become reality. In 1929, African American army pilot William Powell opened the Bessie Coleman Aero Club in Los Angeles.

YUSRA MARDINI

SWIMMER

(b.1998)

A gifted swimmer from Damascus, Syria, Yusra Mardini became an Olympic athlete against all odds. After the Syrian Civil War broke out in 2011, Yusra's home city was repeatedly bombed. Still, she continued to train and in 2012 she represented her country at the World Swimming Championships.

Three years later, Yusra and her sister fled Syria. When the engine of the boat carrying them broke down, they jumped into the sea and pushed it, together with another refugee. Their heroic swim to safety took more than three hours. The Mardini sisters eventually found a new

home in Berlin, Germany. In 2016, Yusra competed at the Olympic Games in Rio, Brazil. Although she didn't win a medal, her story was an inspiration to people everywhere.

"The most important thing in my life is swimming. Then speaking and doing things to help refugees."

TEREZINHA GUILHERMINA
Sprinter
(b.1978)

Often described as the fastest blind woman in the world, the Brazilian Paralympian Terezinha Guilhermina was born with a disease that slowly destroyed her eyesight. Five of her 12 brothers have the same condition.

When Terezinha was 22, she joined a training program for disabled athletes in her home city of Betim. At first she swam, because she couldn't afford running shoes. After her sister gave her a pair, Terezinha took up sprinting. Since then she has competed in four Paralympic Games and achieved world records for different races in her category T11, which is for totally blind athletes. She sprints blindfolded, alongside a sighted guide runner.

"I promised myself to keep training hard and run faster to become the best sprinter in the world. I didn't want to struggle to buy shoes or my favorite foods anymore."

KRYSTYNA SKARBEK
WARTIME SPY
(1908–1952)

Known as Winston Churchill's "number one spy," Krystyna Skarbek (who later changed her name to Christine Granville) was a Polish countess. She moved to Britain after Germany invaded her country in September 1939, causing the outbreak of World War II. Determined to join the fight against Germany, Krystyna entered the British Secret Service, or SOE. She was its first female special agent and its longest-serving one.

Krystyna was brave, daring, and dedicated to protecting her new home country. On one mission she skied out of German-occupied Poland with evidence that the Nazis were planning to invade Soviet Russia hidden in her glove. She also helped in the fight to free France. Krystyna was awarded the George Cross, an OBE, and the Croix de Guerre for her courage and service.

"She was a remarkable woman, it is ludicrous that she is not better known... [H]er story is incredible and she has just not been honored as she should be."

- Clare Mulley, biographer

ANNE BONNY

Pirate

(c.1698–c.1782)

"In all these Expeditions, Anne Bonny bore him Company, and when any Business was to be done in their Way, no Body was more forward or couragious than she..."

- from *A General History of the Pyrates* by Captain Charles Johnson, 1724.

Anne Cormac was born in Ireland, but her parents soon emigrated to the United States. When Anne was 13, her mother died of typhoid fever. Against her father's will, Anne married a pirate called James Bonny when she was 16, but the relationship didn't last.

Anne was very unconventional. She left her husband to join the ship of a pirate called Calico Jack. Pirating was a man's world, but Anne was so daring that she won the respect of the all-male crew. Eventually, in 1720, the authorities caught up with Anne's ship. The whole crew was sentenced to death by hanging. However, Anne's life was spared because she was pregnant. After her release, Anne decided to stop being a pirate and live a quiet, law-abiding life.

AMNA AL HADDAD
WEIGHTLIFTER
(b.1989)

A simple walk in the park changed Amna Al Haddad's life. She was 19 at the time, suffering from depression, and taking antidepressants. She ate junk food, never exercised, slept 12 hours a day, and didn't have any friends. Amna is open about how she felt: "I was at one of the lowest points in my life, with no hope that the future could be better."

She couldn't go on as she was, so Amna decided to change. She went for a walk around nearby Safa Park on the outskirts of her home city, Dubai, United Arab Emirates (UAE). Amna's next step was to join a gym. As soon as she tried weightlifting, she loved it. It was perfect for making her more resilient, or able to bounce back. As Amna's physical health improved, so did her mental well-being.

Building up her strength wasn't Amna's biggest challenge. Dubai has a strict code of conduct based on Islamic laws. For a long time it was taboo for women to take part in sports. They were only allowed to be weightlifters beginning in 2000. Amna had such passion for her chosen sport that she was ready to challenge convention and show that Muslim women can be powerful athletes.

By 2012, just five years after taking up weightlifting, Amna was ranked 77th out of 170 women in Asia after she competed in the Reebok Crossfit Games Open. She set herself an ambitious goal—to represent the UAE in the 2016 Rio Olympics.

Amna gave up her job as a journalist to be a full-time weightlifter. Whenever she competed, she made headlines. She was often the only Emirati to compete or the first woman in a hijab.

In 2015, Amna won six gold medals and three silver medals in the International

Weightlifting Federation (IWF) Asian Interclub Championships. Nike offered her a sponsorship deal and she worked with the brand to develop its first sport hijab. Amna applauded Nike for making sports more accessible to Muslim girls and women who chose to wear the hijab as a sign of modesty. At the same time, she also made it clear that she supported all Muslim sportswomen, whether they wore the hijab or not.

Amna qualified for the Rio Games, but had to pull out because of an injury to her lower back. However, her example has inspired more Muslim women and girls to follow their dreams. Through her honesty, Amna has removed some of the stigma around depression. She is also living proof that exercise is a fantastic way to improve mental health.

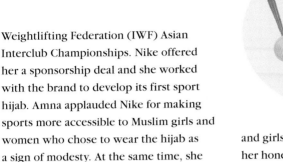

"Women have the right to choose what to wear as athletes, and religious beliefs should never be a barrier to pursuing sports."

JESSICA WATSON

Sailor and Writer

(b.1993)

In May 2010, thousands of people gathered at Sydney Harbor, Australia, to welcome home an extraordinary teenager. Sailor Jessica Watson, then 16 years old, was returning from a 210-day solo journey around the world. She was the youngest person to sail nonstop around the world.

"You don't have to be someone special to achieve something big. You just have to have a dream, believe in it, and work hard."

Some people criticized Jessica's parents for letting her go, especially since she had crashed into a freighter (large ship) during a test run. There were also concerns about how Jessica would cope with being alone for so long.

Jessica faced challenging moments. During one especially vicious storm, the wind picked up her yacht *Ella's Pink Lady* and threw it into the base of a towering wave. The boat was knocked onto its side at least seven times during the journey.

In 2011, Jessica was named Young Australian of the Year. She is a Youth Ambassador for the United Nations' World Food Programme (WFP), which works to end hunger.

Jessica wrote a blog, which was read by people around the globe. She documented her difficulties, but also described the amazing wildlife she encountered. The supportive messages that she received from her followers really helped to boost her morale. After she returned home, Jessica wrote a book about her experiences called *True Spirit*.

MARINA RASKOVA
War Pilot and Navigator
(1912–1943)

When Marina Malinina was growing up in Moscow, Russia, she dreamed of following in her father's footsteps and becoming an opera singer. But her ambitions changed while she was at school and she focused on chemistry instead. Marina left high school in 1929, seven years after her country had become part of the Soviet Union. Marina worked as a chemist in a dye factory, met an engineer named Sergei Raskov, and married.

In 1931, Marina went to work for the Soviet Air Force. She became its first female navigator. In 1934, Marina became the first woman to teach at the Zhukovsky Air Academy in Moscow. She also set many long-distance flying records. In 1938, Marina was one of the first women to receive a Hero of the Soviet Union award.

After World War II had started, Marina called for women to be allowed to fly as military pilots. As a result, the women's flying corps was formed. It was made up of three regiments, each containing about 400 women—mechanics, engineers, and navigators, as well as pilots.

Marina commanded the dive-bombing regiment until she died in battle in 1943. She was given a state funeral in recognition of her bravery, and was later awarded the Order of Patriotic War 1st Class.

MARINA RASKOVA URGES THE SOVIET LEADER JOSEPH STALIN TO ALLOW WOMEN PILOTS, SEPTEMBER 1941:

"You know, they are running away to the front all the same—they are taking things into their own hands—and it will be worse, you understand, if they steal planes to go."

GERTRUDE BELL
Diplomat, Spy, Archaeologist, Mountaineer, and Writer
(1868–1926)

Gertrude Margaret Lowthian Bell was born into a wealthy family in County Durham, England. Her mother died when she was three years old, and her father remarried when she was seven. Gertrude's parents encouraged her to go to university, which was unusual at the time. She studied modern history at Lady Margaret Hall, one of Oxford University's first women's colleges, and was awarded a first-class degree.

In 1892, Gertrude visited her uncle, who was a British diplomat in Tehran, Persia (now Iran). She had learned to speak Persian and translated a book of Persian poetry into English and wrote her first travel book, *Persian Pictures*.

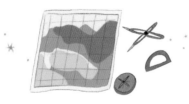

Gertrude became an avid and fearless climber. In 1902, she became stuck in a blizzard while scaling the highest peak in the Swiss Alps, the Finsteraarhorn. She earned the respect of mountaineers after she survived dangling off a rope for two days. The 8,635 feet (2,632 m) Gertrudespitze is named after her.

Gertrude learned the language wherever she went, got to know the local politics, and wrote letters home about what she did and saw. Over her lifetime, Gertrude became fluent in eight languages. She also taught herself archaeology and was involved in digs in the Ottoman Empire (in the middle of which is now Turkey), Syria, and Mesopotamia (now Iraq). She was becoming an expert on the Middle East.

During World War I, Gertrude worked for the British Intelligence office in Cairo, Egypt, along with T.E. Lawrence ("Lawrence of Arabia"). Her familiarity with Arabic language, culture, and politics meant she could influence the events in the region to suit the British government.

"It's so nice to be a spoke in the wheel, one that helps to turn, not one that hinders."

The British had encouraged Arabs in the region to revolt against Ottoman rule. After the war, Gertrude was one of the experts who sat on the panel to decide the new borders within the territory. She was a driving force behind the creation of Iraq and its first king in 1921.

In 1923, Gertrude stepped down from politics and diplomacy to focus on another passion—archaeology. Between 1923 and 1926, she established what is now the National Museum of Iraq and was its first director. Gertrude wanted

NATIONAL MUSEUM OF IRAQ

the Iraqis to be able to keep archeological finds from the Sumerian, Babylonian, and Assyrian civilizations in their own country.

Gertrude is relatively unknown in her home country now, but she is held in high esteem in Iraq. After her death in 1926, she was buried in Baghdad and her grave there has been visited ever since. Many families in the Iraqi capital refer to Gertrude fondly as the "first lady of Iraq."

MiSTY COPELAND
PRiNCiPAL BALLERiNA
(b.1982)

Combining athleticism, technique, and emotion, ballet is incredibly demanding. Countless dancers strive to become professional, but only the tiniest number are successful. Among those is Misty Danielle Copeland, the first African American to be made principal dancer at the American Ballet Theatre (ABT) in New York City.

Misty was born in Kansas City, but moved to San Francisco with her mother and five brothers and sisters when she was still very young. She never knew her father, and often struggled with her mother's partners. She lived in poverty.

When Misty was 13, she auditioned for the school dance team. After performing her own choreography, she was named the captain of the 60-member squad. Her coach, who had a background in classical dance, recommended that Misty try some ballet classes.

Misty wasn't convinced that she would enjoy ballet, but she enrolled. For the first few weeks she had no clue what she was supposed to be doing, but her instructor, Cindy Bradley, saw her huge potential at once.

Most professional dancers start training at the age of three. From her uncertain, late start, Misty progressed to attending

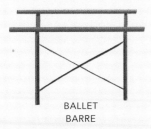

BALLET
BARRE

five classes a week. Within three months she could dance *en pointe*—a technique that takes most dancers years to master.

Cindy knew Misty's background was very poor, so she didn't charge to teach her ballet. When Misty's mother moved and it became impossible for her to travel back and forth between home, school, and ballet classes, Cindy invited Misty into her home during the week, and then Misty saw her mother on the weekends.

When Misty was 15, she won first place at the Los Angeles Music Center Spotlight Awards. Later that year she was awarded a full scholarship to the San Francisco Ballet's six-week summer course. In 1999 and 2000, Misty won scholarships to attend the ABT's summer school. She was one of six dancers (out of 150) who were asked to join the ABT's junior troupe. Misty soon rose to fame. In 2007, she became the ABT's first African American soloist and in 2015 she

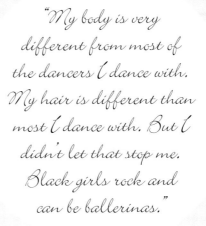

"My body is very different from most of the dancers I dance with. My hair is different than most I dance with. But I didn't let that stop me. Black girls rock and can be ballerinas."

became a principal (the highest rank of dancer).

Misty has become an icon of popular culture. In 2016, she was the model for one of the Barbie "Sheroes" collection. The doll wore a copy of the red unitard Misty wore in the ballet *Firebird*. Misty also starred in Disney's *The Nutcracker and the Four Realms* (2018) as the Ballerina.

Misty supports many charitable organizations and regularly mentors young dancers.

SACAGAWEA
EXPLORER AND INTERPRETER
(c.1788–1812)

Sacagawea was a Native American from the Shoshone tribe. When she was 11 or 12, she was captured by a party of the Hidatsa tribe and taken to their settlement. A few years later, the French Canadian explorer and fur trader Toussaint Charbonneau bought Sacagawea and made her one of his many wives.

In 1804, explorers Meriwether Lewis and William Clark hired Toussaint as a guide. They were going on an expedition to map the West for President Thomas Jefferson.

Lewis and Clark asked Toussaint to bring along Sacagawea as an interpreter. They set off in March 1805, just a few weeks after Sacagawea had given birth to a son, Jean Baptiste. She carried her baby with her in a cradleboard.

"Everything I do is for my people."

Sacagawea was a huge help on the expedition. As well as making it possible for the group to communicate and trade with the Shoshone, she could tell them which roots and plants were edible. She even made them moccasins to wear. On one occasion she rescued Lewis and Clark's journals from a river.

Sacagawea is celebrated to this day. Numerous statues of her stand along the expedition trail. Her image also features on a collectable golden dollar coin produced in 2000.

MARY KOM

Boxer

(b.1983)

Nicknamed "MC Mary Kom" and "Magnificent Mary," Mangte Chungneijang Mary Kom was born in rural Manipur, a state in northeastern India. The oldest of three children, she helped her parents out in the rice fields. The family was very poor and sometimes they had nothing to eat.

When Mary saw footage of the legendary American boxer Muhammad Ali on television, she was inspired to take up the sport. She trained in secret, because her father had strict ideas about what girls should and shouldn't do.

"Don't let anyone tell you you're weak because you're a woman."

In 2000, Mary won the state boxing championship. Her father read about her victory in the papers, but he didn't start to accept and support her choice of career for another three years. Mary won her first World Amateur Boxing Championship in 2002 and her first Asian Women's Boxing Championship the following year.

In 2012, Mary became the first female Indian boxer to qualify for the Olympic Games. She returned home with a bronze medal, and went on to win gold in the 2018 Commonwealth Games.

Mary has set up an academy to teach boxing to children from poor backgrounds in Manipur and other parts of India.

OLYMPIC BRONZE

NOOR INAYAT KHAN
Writer and Spy
(1914–1944)

In wartime, countries rely on spies—secret agents who adopt false identities, cross enemy lines, and find out inside information that might help win the war. Noor Inayat Khan was a fearless, intelligent, and conscientious spy who worked for Britain during World War II.

Born in Moscow, Russia, Noor was exposed to many cultures as she was growing up. Her father was an Indian Muslim and her mother was an American. During Noor's childhood, her family moved to London and then Paris, where Noor was educated. She studied music and medicine and was bilingual in French and English.

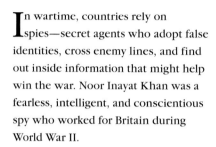

BIG BEN, LONDON

In 1939, Noor worked on a collection of Indian children's stories, which were published in the newspaper *Le Figaro*. When war broke out, she decided to train as a nurse with the French Red Cross. Shortly before France surrendered to Germany in November 1940, Noor fled to England with her mother and sister.

Noor's father, a Sufi mystic, had raised her to believe in peace and religious harmony. Noor was determined to work against fascist Germany and support efforts to end the war. She joined the Women's Auxiliary Air Force (WAAF)

in 1940 as a radio operator. She was soon noticed by Special Operation Executive (SOE) agents and recruited in 1942.

In 1943, Noor was sent to work for a resistance network in Paris. Her job was to radio any intelligence (information) back to London. Soon after she arrived, many women in the network were arrested. Noor's bosses urged her to return home. However, she insisted on staying. She wanted to gather as much information as she could before she was found out.

EIFFEL TOWER, PARIS

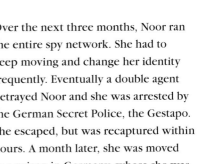

"Liberté!"
(Freedom!)

NOOR'S LAST WORD
AS SHE WAS SHOT

Over the next three months, Noor ran the entire spy network. She had to keep moving and change her identity frequently. Eventually a double agent betrayed Noor and she was arrested by the German Secret Police, the Gestapo. She escaped, but was recaptured within hours. A month later, she was moved to a prison in Germany, where she was chained and kept in solitary confinement.

Despite repeated torture and starvation, Noor never volunteered any information to her captors. After 10 months, she was moved to the concentration camp at Dachau, where she was killed by firing squad. After her death, Noor was awarded the Croix de Guerre and the George Cross for her bravery.

WAAF RADIO

CHANTAL PETITCLERC
Wheelchair Racer and Senator
(b.1969)

Until Chantal Petitclerc was 13 years old, her life was similar to that of many children in her home town of Saint-Marc-des-Carrières, Canada. Then one day Chantal was playing on a friend's farm when an old barn door fell onto her, breaking her spine.

When Chantal was released from the hospital, she was in a wheelchair. She had lost the use of her legs because she was paralyzed from the hips down. Her physical education teacher offered her lunchtime swimming lessons to increase her upper body strength.

Chantal enjoyed the challenge and continued her swimming lessons until she graduated from school. Chantal

went on to Université Laval in Quebec City, where she was introduced to wheelchair athletics. She took part in her first competition and even though she came last, she was hooked. She continued to train while she completed her university studies, and in 1992 she qualified for the Barcelona Paralympic Games. She brought home two bronze medals.

Over the next 16 years, Chantal won more medals than any other Canadian track athlete or sportsperson. She was the only athlete to win gold medals in the Olympic Games, Paralympic Games, and Commonwealth Games. This was possible because wheelchair racing was included in the 2004 Olympics as well as the Paralympics.

Chantal has won a total of 21 Paralympic medals (14 golds) and broken 26 world records. In the 2004 Paralympics she won five gold medals—matching the record for a single Games (set by the Canadian swimmer Stephanie

> *"I believe in the power of sport to change lives, to make people better, and to empower."*

Dixon at the 2000 Paralympics). Chantal was chosen to carry the flag at the start of the 2006 Commonwealth Games, which took place in Melbourne, Australia.

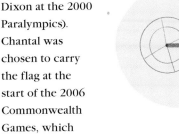

Chantal retired from wheelchair racing after the 2008 Beijing Olympics. Since then she has been a coach and mentor for the British Paralympic teams and Chef de Mission (person in charge) for the Canadian teams at the Commonwealth and Paralympic Games.

Chantal is an ambassador for Right to Play, an international organization that educates children through play to help them overcome trauma and poverty. She also supports the Champions Fund, which gives grants to support promising Canadian female athletes, teams, and tournaments.

Chantal has been awarded honorary doctorates from universities across Canada and the Lou Marsh Trophy for Canadian Athlete of the Year. She was admitted into the Paralympic Hall of Fame in 2016. That same year, she started to serve as a senator for the Canadian government.

CANADIAN SENATE

ALEXANDRA DAVID-NÉEL
EXPLORER AND WRITER
(1868–1969)

Alexandra David-Néel was an adventurous child, often wandering off through the busy streets of her home city of Paris, France. She converted to Buddhism at 21 years old and this inspired her later travels across India, Japan, and China. In the winter of 1924, Alexandra crossed the Himalayas to Llasa, Tibet. The city was forbidden to foreigners, but she was able to enter it disguised as a beggar. Alexandra returned to Tibet in 1938 and studied Buddhism there for five years.

Alexandra lived to be almost 101. She spent the last 20 years of her life in France and Monaco writing about her travels. According to her wishes, her ashes were scattered in the River Ganges in Varanasi, India.

"To the one who knows how to look and feel, every moment of this free wandering life is an enchantment."

NATALIE DU TOIT

Swimmer

(b.1984)

"I don't think of myself as being disabled, or able-bodied. I just want to be myself and go for my own dreams and goals."

Natalie du Toit was already a successful competitive swimmer when she lost the lower half of her left leg in a car accident at the age of 17. Determined to continue her sporting career, she returned to the pool after four months. She decided to compete as a Paralympian for her home country, South Africa.

Natalie was soon winning medals and breaking world records. In 2008, she was one of two Paralympians who qualified for both the Olympic and Paralympic Games. Over the course of her career, Natalie has won more than 18 gold medals. She retired from the sport in 2012.

STARTING BLOCK

JUNKO TABEI
Mountaineer and Environmentalist
(1939–2016)

Junko Tabei was the first woman to reach the summit of Mount Everest, as well as climb the highest peaks on all seven of the world's continents. Junko's husband, who was also a climber, supported her ambition.

Junko founded Japan's first women's climbing club in 1969. Her ascent of Everest took place in May 1975. She continued to climb mountains until the end of her life. Junko worried about damage to Everest, so she returned to university in her sixties to complete a postgraduate degree in environmental science. She worked to protect and preserve delicate mountain environments.

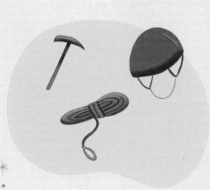

"I love to go wherever I've never been before. So I am challenging myself to climb all the highest peaks of all countries of the world. I am now 76, and have scaled the highest peaks of 76 countries."

MAJLINDA KELMENDI
Judoka (Judo Master)
(b.1991)

Majlinda Kelmendi is from Kosovo, a European state that was formed in 2008 from territory that had been part of Serbia. She started judo training at age eight. In 2009, she won the gold medal at the World Junior Championships in Paris.

Majlinda took part in the 2012 London Olympics but she had to represent Albania—Kosovo was not yet recognized by the Olympic Committee. She achieved her first gold medal for Kosovo at the 2013 World Judo Championships. In the 2016 Rio Olympics, Majlinda made history by winning Kosovo's first Olympic gold. She returned home a national hero. She has also won three gold medals in the European Championships. She competes in the 52-kg (115 lb) weight category.

"I started to really like judo because I made new friends, I saw new cities, and I realized that this was a way for me to really be somebody."

AMELIA EARHART

AVIATOR

(1897–c.1937)

There are many competing stories about the end of American aviator Amelia Earhart's life. She and navigator Fred Noonan sparked a huge search when they went missing above the Pacific Ocean in July 1937. Not a trace of them was found—and no trace of the Lockheed Model 10-E Electra aircraft they were flying was found either. Exactly what happened to Amelia and Fred remains a mystery to this day.

Amelia was born in Kansas. In 1917, just after starting university in Pennsylvania, she visited her sister in Toronto, Canada. Wounded soldiers were returning from World War I and Amelia was moved to help. Instead of returning to university, she volunteered at the military hospital.

In 1918, Amelia caught the Spanish flu that was sweeping across the world and would end up killing up to 100 million people. Amelia was hospitalized for two months and had to rest for almost a year. Amelia suffered from sinus problems for the rest of her life.

In 1920, Amelia went to live with her parents in California. It was here that she first flew in a plane. Amelia was so thrilled by the experience that she decided to take flying lessons. In 1921, her mother and sister helped her to buy her first plane, and by 1923 Amelia was a fully qualified pilot.

"The woman who can create her own job is the woman who will win fame and fortune."

In 1928, some promoters asked Amelia if she would be the first woman on a flight across the Atlantic Ocean. The plane was being piloted by two men so she would just be a passenger. Amelia agreed and returned a hero. She released a best-selling book, *20 Hrs 40 Min* (the time the flight took), went on a lecture tour across the United States, and was able to make money by being the "face" of various products and brands.

Wanting to justify her fame, Amelia made a transatlantic solo flight in 1932. She completed the crossing in record time, despite various difficulties along the way. This was the beginning of a series of record-breaking flights and historical firsts. In 1932, she became the first woman to receive the Distinguished Flying Cross, and in 1935 she was the first person to fly solo from Hawaii to the US mainland.

Amelia was one of the pilots who founded the Ninety-Nines in 1929, an organization in which women pilots offered each other mutual support. She also designed a clothing line for women who "lived actively."

DISTINGUISHED FLYING CROSS

When Amelia went missing, she had almost completed a pioneering around-the-world flight. She had packed a lot of living into her 40 years of life.

SIMONE BILES
GYMNAST
(b.1997)

Simone Arianne Biles is one of the most gifted gymnasts in sporting history. She is celebrated globally, but her road to success wasn't easy.

Born in Ohio, Simone was two years old when she and three siblings were taken into foster care because their mother was struggling with alcohol and drug addiction. When she was six, Simone was adopted by her biological grandparents in Texas. Today she sees them as her parents.

Around this time, Simone joined a gymnastics class after a teacher noticed her talent on a school trip. She was a natural and progressed very quickly.

SPRINGBOARD

Simone was spotted at the age of eight by the gymnastics coach Aimee Boorman, who has been her trainer ever since. Aimee has given Simone much-needed support, especially during the

tougher phases of her training when she struggled with flexibility and wasn't performing as well.

VAULT

In 2011, when Simone was 14 years old, she had to make one of the biggest decisions of her life—did she want to become a full-time professional gymnast, training 32 hours over six days every week, or did she want to lead a regular teenage life and miss out on being an elite athlete?

"I'd rather regret the risks that didn't work out than the chances I didn't take at all"

Determined to become a world-class gymnast, Simone opted for intensive training and homeschooling. At first her results were outstanding, and she started to make a name for herself. But in 2013, she injured herself repeatedly during a championship, tripping, falling, and making mistakes. Aimee pulled her from the competition.

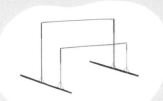

UNEVEN BARS

Simone's parents decided to enlist the help of a sports psychologist, who helped Simone work through what may have been anxiety about performing. An incredible three weeks later, she won the US Championships—two months after that she was awarded a world title.

Simone made history by becoming the first woman to win 10 gold medals in the World Championships (across 2013, 2014, and 2015). She also holds the most World Championship medals of any American gymnast.

In 2016, Simone made her Olympic debut in Rio. She returned home with four gold medals (for the individual all-around, vault, floor, and team categories). She also won a bronze for the balance beam. Simone took a well-earned rest from training in 2017 before returning to the world of gymnastics in 2018.

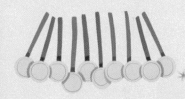

As well as setting new, extremely high standards in gymnastics, Simone dedicates time to charities that are close to her heart. She wants children in foster care to have the support and opportunities to realize their potential. She also works with Kids Wish, which makes dreams come true for children with terminal illnesses.

QUIZ

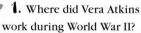

1. Where did Vera Atkins work during World War II?

2. What was the first club that Marta played soccer for at age 14?

3. What are the names of the two tennis-playing sisters whose careers have included two Career Golden Slams?

4. What type of pilot did Bessie Coleman decide to be?

5. Where did Yusra Mardini and her sister find a home after leaving Syria?

6. What sport did Terezinha Guilhermina try before sprinting?

7. Where did Krystyna Skarbek once hide vital information about a Nazi invasion?

8. What was the profession of Anne Bonny?

9. What did Amna Al Haddad help sports brand Nike to develop, the first of its kind?

10. What was the name of Jessica Watson's yacht?

11. What award did Marina Raskova receive in 1938?

12. How many languages did Gertrude Bell become fluent in over her lifetime?

13. Which Native American tribe was Sacagawea from?

14. What medal did Mary Kom win at the 2018 Commonwealth Games?

15. How many world records has Chantal Petitclerc broken?

16. What organization was founded by aviator Amelia Earhart?

Answers: 1. France; 2. Vasco da Gama club; 3. Venus and Serena Williams; 4. barnstormer; 5. Berlin, Germany; 6. swimming; 7. glove; 8. pirate; 9. hijab; 10. Ella's Pink Lady; 11. Hero of the Soviet Union Award; 12. eight; 13. Shoshone; 14. gold; 15. 26; 16. the Ninety-Nines.

RESEARCH PROJECT!

Now that you have read about all of these inspiring women, it's time to take a look closer to home. The women in your life have incredible stories to tell, too!

Speak to your mom, aunt, grandmother, caregiver, or teacher to discover their stories and their own experiences. Here are some questions to get you started:

WHO WERE YOUR FEMALE HEROES GROWING UP?

WHAT ACHIEVEMENT ARE YOU MOST PROUD OF?

WHO HAS SUPPORTED YOU THROUGH YOUR LIFE?

HAVE YOU OVERCOME DIFFICULTIES TO ACHIEVE YOUR GOALS?

WHICH WOMEN DO YOU ADMIRE TODAY?

WHAT ARE THE MOST IMPORTANT LESSONS THAT YOU HAVE LEARNED?

WHAT IS THE BEST JOB YOU HAVE HAD?

WHAT ADVICE WOULD YOU GIVE YOUNG WOMEN TODAY?

AS A CHILD, WHAT DID YOU WANT TO BE WHEN YOU GREW UP?

HOW WAS YOUR EXPERIENCE IN SCHOOL?

WHERE DID YOU GROW UP?

Listen carefully to the answers that people give. It is important to record information correctly when people are speaking. If you are going to record what someone tells you, make sure that you ask permission first.

When you have finished asking questions, you can write a report about the person you talked to. You could even include a portrait of them!

Remember that some people might not want to answer one or more of your questions. If that's the case, be respectful and move on to the next question, or simply ask someone else who is willing to share their story. If you want to record their answers, you must ask for permission first.

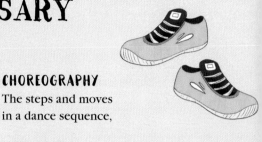

GLOSSARY

CHOREOGRAPHY
The steps and moves in a dance sequence,

CIVIL WAR
A war between citizens of the same country.

ABOLISH
Put an end to a system or practice, such as slavery.

CONSCIENTIOUS
Hard working and wishing to fulfill your duty well and thoroughly.

ANTIDEPRESSANTS
A drug or medicine used to relieve depression.

CONVENTION
The way that something is usually done.

ARCHAEOLOGIST
Someone who studies history through looking at objects from the past.

COURAGE
Being able to do something that frightens you; bravery.

AUTOIMMUNE DISEASE
Illness caused by the body's defense system attacking the body's own substances.

DIPLOMACY
Managing the relations between countries.

AVIATION
The science and practice of flying an aircraft.

DISCRIMINATION
An unfair system that treats people differently, for example because of their sex, race, sexuality, or age.

AVIATOR
Someone who flies and operates an aircraft.

EMIGRATE
To leave one's own country and settle permanently in another.

BUDDHISM
A religion founded in India in the 5th century BC by Siddhartha Gautama.

FRAILTY
Weakness or lack of strength.

GHETTO
An area within a town or city that is occupied by a group of people who are in the minority of the population.

INFERIOR
Lower in quality or status.

INTERPRETER
Someone who translates the language spoken by one person so that another can understand.

ISLAMIC LAWS
The rules of the Muslim religion, also called Sharia.

MAIDEN NAME
A woman's original surname, this may change when she marries if she takes her husband's surname.

NAVIGATOR
Someone who plans the course that an aircraft, ship, or car will take.

PARALYMPIAN
Someone who competes in the Paralympic Games, an international sports festival for athletes with disabilities.

POVERTY
A state poorness.

RACIST
Views that are unfair and based on racial prejudice, or someone who believes that one race is superior to another.

SANITATION
Services that keep a place clean, such as water and sewage systems in a town.

SEGREGATION
Separating people into groups, usually according to their race.

SINUS
A system of cavities in bones or tissue, usually the cavities in your forehead and cheeks that connect with the nasal passages.

SPECIMEN
An animal, plant. or other item taken to show an example of its type.

STIGMA
A mark of disgrace associated with a person, place, or circumstance.

TABOO
A practice that is forbidden by social or religious custom.

TYPHOID FEVER
A bacterial infection that shows as red spots on the chest and abdomen and causes severe sickness.

UNCONVENTIONAL
Not following what is generally done or believed.

FURTHER INFORMATION

BOOKS

ANTHOLOGY OF AMAZING WOMEN
by Sandra Lawrence and Nathan Collins (20 Watt, 2018)

F IS FOR FEMINISM by Carolyn Suzuki (Ladybird, 2019)

FANTASTICALLY GREAT WOMEN WHO CHANGED THE WORLD
by Kate Pankhurst (Bloomsbury Children's Books, 2016)

GIRLS CAN DO ANYTHING! by Caryl Hart (Scholastic, 2018)

GIRLS WHO CHANGED THE WORLD
by Michelle Roehm McCann (Simon & Schuster, 2018)

HER STORY: 50 WOMEN AND GIRLS WHO SHOOK THE WORLD
by Katherine Halligan (Nosy Crow, 2018)

I KNOW A WOMAN: THE INSPIRING CONNECTIONS BETWEEN THE WOMEN WHO HAVE CHANGED OUR WORLD
by Kate Hodges (Aurum Press, 2018)

INCREDIBLE SPORTING CHAMPIONS (BRILLIANT WOMEN)
by Georgia Amson-Bradshaw (Wayland, 2019)

SPORTOPEDIA: EXPLORE MORE THAN 50 SPORTS FROM AROUND THE WORLD
by Adam Skinner (Wide Eyed Editions, 2018)

TRUE SPIRIT: THE AUSSIE GIRL WHO TOOK ON THE WORLD
by Jessica Watson (Hachette Australia, 2011)

WOMEN IN SPORT: FIFTY FEARLESS ATHLETES WHO PLAYED TO WIN
by Rachel Ignotofsky (Wren & Rook, 2018)

YOUNG, GIFTED AND BLACK: MEET 52 BLACK HEROES FROM PAST AND PRESENT
by Jamia Wilson (Wide Eyed Editions, 2018)

WEBSITES

The Amazing Women in History website aims
to bring together all the amazing women
left out of history books.
amazingwomeninhistory.com/

The Inspirational Women Series website displays
a series of interviews with women leaders
from around the world.
inspirationalwomenseries.org/

Have a look at the section on Women Who
Made History on the English Heritage website.
english-heritage.org.uk/learn/histories/women-in-history/

Find out who has won the prestigious Nobel Peace Prize.
nobelpeaceprize.org/

Find audio clips of Vera Atkins at the Imperial War Museum.
iwm.org.uk/collections/item/object/80009338

Take a look at the history of the Women's Auxiliary Air Force.
bbc.co.uk/history/ww2peopleswar/timeline/factfiles/nonflash/a6649932.shtml

Check out the FIFA site to see
the Best FIFA Women's Players.
fifa.com/the-best-fifa-football-awards/
best-fifa-womens-player/

Have a look through Jessica Watson's
website to find out more about her.
jessicawatson.com.au

Learn more about Misty Copeland
at her website.
mistycopeland.com/

Find out more about Simone Biles'
amazing achievements on her website.
simonebiles.com/

INDEX